In The Land Of The Great White Castle

Words by Norman C. Habel
Pictures by Jim Roberts

Concordia Publishing House

℗ A PURPLE PUZZLE TREE BOOK

COPYRIGHT © 1971
CONCORDIA PUBLISHING HOUSE,
ST. LOUIS, MISSOURI
CONCORDIA PUBLISHING HOUSE LTD.,
LONDON, E. C. 1
MANUFACTURED IN THE
UNITED STATES OF AMERICA
ALL RIGHTS RESERVED
ISBN 0-570-06504-6

When Noah died
his children cried,
and his grandchildren cried,
and his great-grandchildren cried.
Everybody cried.
But not for very long!
For they couldn't help laughing
at the wild story
that Noah had told
about the dirty purple waters
which covered the land
when God split the world in two.
Of course,
they thought it wasn't true.
Well, do you?

When Noah was dead,
the people were bored.
So they yawned
and they sneered.
And they laughed
and they snored.

They lived in a land called Babylon,
a land of tall white castles
with beautiful golden towers.
It was a land of shining temples
with beautiful silver walls.
They built those shining temples
for all their goofy gods.
Their gods had heads
that looked like bulls
or snakes or fish,
or great big ugly frogs.

Then the people had a meeting,
for they were very sassy
and very, very bored.
One guy said, "Good heavens!"
And one guy said, "Good lord,
it's time that we were famous.
Why shouldn't people honor us
if they honor nutty Noah?
He's only a goofy old goat,
who built a funny old boat
and turned it into a zoo!"

Soon they all decided
to build an enormous castle
with a tower on the top,
where gods could stop
to laugh and dance and play.

All the people wanted
a great white shining castle
like a station out in space,
very, very high.
There the gods could have a picnic
in front of heaven's gates.
And men could come to spy
on all their goofy gods,
who stopped to play
at that castle in the sky.

They started to build
with big white bricks
that soon became a tower.
They built it higher
and higher
and higher
and higher,
trying to reach the
gate of heaven.

But the gate of heaven is very high,
very, very, very high.
Then one bright morning
God looked down
to see just what was up.
He squinted and peered
at the earth below.
Alas, He could hardly see
that big white castle
way down there!
It looked so very tiny,
and so very far away!
God knew quite well
what those sassy men had planned.
So He said to Himself,
"I must teach them all a lesson,
and punish the world again."

"I'll tangle their tongues
and then there'll be fun
when they try to talk to each other.
Some will talk in Chinese
or maybe old Hindu.
Some will talk like an Indian chief
or a native from Timbuktoo.
And when they all chatter,
there'll be such a clatter
they'll sound like birds in a zoo."

Next morning they started
to build once again,
but nobody knew what to do.
For some talked in Chinese
and some in old Hindu.
When everyone talked
and everyone squawked,
they sounded like birds in a zoo.

So the tower was never finished
and the people went away,
as far as they could go.
They wanted a place to live and die
far away from God.

A long time passed
and it seemed as though
God had forgotten the world.
He seemed to be lost forever.
I wonder whether
God will ever
put His puzzle
back together
once again!
What do you think He'll do?

Well, one of the families
who stayed behind
in the land of the big white castle
had a favorite son called Abraham.
And one fine day
he ran away from home,
away from the mighty land
of the big white shining castle.

And if you ask him why,
he probably will say:
"I ran away
because God said,
'Now Abraham, My boy,
you have to leave
this mighty land
and run away from home.
You have to take
a long, long trip
to a strange land
that'll really make you flip!'"

So Abraham left his home that day,
but he didn't know where he was going.
And that seems rather silly,
don't you think?

After a while
Abraham came to a hillbilly land,
a really hilly hillbilly land,
a land that God called Canaan.
And in that land
of rocks and sand
Abraham watched his cattle.
For he was like a hillbilly man
of long, long ago.

Then God said to Abraham,
"I'm starting a brand-new puzzle
that will take
a long, long time to finish.
We're starting at the bottom
where you fit next to Me.
You're to be the first big piece
in My brand-new purple puzzle.
Well, do you agree?"

Abraham said, "O.K."
And God said, quietly,
"What this means, My boy,
    is that you will have some children.
    And they'll have children too.

And everyone who trusts in Me,
because he sticks to you,
will make that puzzle grow
and grow and grow into a mighty puzzle tree.
As I set more pieces of the puzzle
carefully in place,
all men will come to see
just how much I love you,
and want you all to trust in Me."

What a picture that will be
when all the parts are set in place,
like the pieces of a purple puzzle tree.

OTHER TITLES

SET I.
WHEN GOD WAS ALL ALONE 56-1200
WHEN THE FIRST MAN CAME 56-1201
IN THE ENCHANTED GARDEN 56-1202
WHEN THE PURPLE WATERS CAME AGAIN 56-1203
IN THE LAND OF THE GREAT WHITE CASTLE 56-1204
WHEN LAUGHING BOY WAS BORN 56-1205
SET I. LP RECORD 79-2200
SET I. GIFT BOX (6 BOOKS, 1 RECORD) 56-1206

SET II.
HOW TRICKY JACOB WAS TRICKED 56-1207
WHEN JACOB BURIED HIS TREASURE 56-1208
WHEN GOD TOLD US HIS NAME 56-1209
IS THAT GOD AT THE DOOR? 56-1210
IN THE MIDDLE OF A WILD CHASE 56-1211
THIS OLD MAN CALLED MOSES 56-1212
SET II. LP RECORD 79-2201
SET II. GIFT BOX (6 BOOKS, 1 RECORD) 56-1213

the PURPLE PUZZLE TREE